Embracing Your Divorce
Navigating Divorce with Grace and Resilience

VERLANDA NACOLE SMITH

Dedication

This book is dedicated to my loving and supportive parents Charles and Jacqueline Smith, my two cubs (Samuel and Amora McSwain), and my entire support system.

Contents

Disclaimer

The author has used her best efforts in preparing this book, she makes no claims to be a licensed counselor, therapist, advisor, or attorney. The advice and strategies contained herein may not be suitable for your situation.

You should consult with a licensed professional where appropriate. Neither the publisher nor author shall be liable for any loss in relationships or mental, emotional, or physical stress, including but not limited to special, incidental, consequential, or other damages.

This book is for informational purposes only. The views expressed are those of the author alone and should not be taken as expert instruction or commands. The reader is responsible for his or her own actions.

Any perceived slight of any individual or organization is purely unintentional.

Preface

First of all, a very warm hug to anybody who has decided to read this book. I understand that reading a book on divorce may not be your idea of a relaxing weekend activity, but if you need to talk to a friend over coffee (or wine!), this is the book for you.

Let us be practical for a moment. Emotions, legalese, and the never-ending stream of "What next?" queries may make going through a divorce seem like being tossed into a blender. While it may seem like a storm right now, a rainbow is at the end of the tunnel. Yes, it is cheesy, but bear with me!

The purpose of "Embracing Your Divorce" is not to languish in the "why me?" phase of recovery. Consider it more like a buddy system. We are going through this together, from sorting out our feelings to rekindling an old interest (Karaoke, anyone?).

Those who are considering reentering the dating scene or who just want more "me-time" may also find useful information here. And parents, figuring all this out while toting around children, I am going to protect you. We are getting down to the nitty-gritty, but there will not be any confusing language; just honest, open discussion.

So, while you peruse these pages, try to picture us gathered in a warm corner, telling tales, offering words of wisdom, and comforting one another that, indeed, the sun will shine bright again. After all, there is always a chance for a fresh start with every conclusion.

Let us pull ourselves up by the bootstraps and laugh our way out of this mess.

Cheers to the excitement of a new chapter!

Introduction

So, here we are, starting a discussion on something that many people would rather avoid divorce. To begin, I want to commend your courage for investigating this, whether you are now experiencing it, have previously gone through it, or are simply curious about it.

Let us see this one from the inside out: Getting a divorce involves more than simply signing some papers and breaking up. It is a roller coaster ride of feelings. It may seem like a downward spiral on certain days. At other times, it is like seeing the approach of a new day filled with optimism. That is some pretty vivid language there, huh? This, however, is the honest truth.

Do you remember how simple everything was when you were a kid? There is hardly much middle ground between good and terrible, joyful, and sad. Now that we are older, though, we know that the middle ground is where life really blossoms. Divorce, like many other major events in life, takes place in the complex shades of grey between black and white. It has the capacity to be both harrowing and freeing, perplexing, and illuminating.

The obvious problem must be addressed as well. As with many other social titles, 'divorcee' carries with it a number of negative connotations. One thing I want you to remember as we go through this book is that your value is independent of any title. You are more than just a part of your story, no matter how important that part may be.

The message of this book is to take everything that has happened to you and learn from it, no matter how wonderful or awful it may have been. Imagine having a lengthy discussion with a trusted confidant; you may expect to feel a wide range of emotions, as well as to have several "aha!" moments and reassurances.

A divorce is not only a formal order; "rather, it is the beginning of a process. The passage of time during this procedure is sometimes equated to walking over a bridge. On the other side of the bridge lies the shattered relationship, with all the emotions of failure and despair that arise as a direct consequence of the breakup. On the other side of this coin is a life that is well-balanced, one in which individuals have made peace with their past and are looking forward with excitement to what the future holds. The actual bridge, on the other hand, is a rickety construction made of ropes and planks with uneven spacing between them. When visitors cautiously make their way across, they experience the fragmentation, anxiety, and uncertainty that accompany any voyage that involves traversing unknown hazards in order to arrive at an unknown destination. Your goal should be to go through the divorce process with the confidence that you can finally declare, "The past is dead, and I'm ready for a new and better life." Having an understanding of the three fundamental phases of divorce can help you do this.

As we go out on our adventure together, keep in mind these words of advice:

"Every sunset is an opportunity to reset."
Richie Norton

As we go further through the text, keep in mind that you are not alone. We are in this together, whether it is navigating the legal tangles, dealing with the raw emotions, or adjusting to life after a separation. Have a drink of your choice, settle down, and we will discuss the highs, the lows, and everything in between.

Chapter 1

Rediscovering and Acknowledging

Sometimes when we least expect it, life has a funny way of flinging us into the furnace of transformation. This may happen at any time. For many people, a divorce is one example of an event that may fundamentally change their lives. It is a catastrophic incident, so naturally people are going to feel an entire range of emotions, including sadness, anger, and finally acceptance. The process of rediscovering oneself and acknowledging one's past may be quite powerful, despite the fact that it may seem to be overpowering.

The legendary bird known as the phoenix has long been seen as a symbol of rejuvenation and fresh beginnings. After the dissolution of their marriage, many people discover a newfound sense of who they are and what they want to do with their lives, similar to the majestic bird that emerges from its ashes. In this chapter, we will not only dig into the rich mythology of the phoenix, but we will also examine human experiences that represent this same process of rebirth after a divorce. These personal stories will be interspersed throughout the chapter.

However, this is not only about making a comeback; it is also about thoroughly comprehending the plethora of feelings that come at a significant turning point in one's life and learning how to navigate through them. It is a process that has to be acknowledged, from the raw, first stages of sorrow and fury to the more reflective times of acceptance. The acceptance of these feelings, as opposed to avoiding or suppressing them, may be therapeutic and pave the path for healing and personal development.

As you continue to read these pages, keep in mind that every account of rediscovery is distinct, and that every feeling is genuine. This chapter serves as a gentle reminder that even in the aftermath of life's most painful times, just like the phoenix, we too have the potential to rise, renew, and reinvent ourselves. This chapter serves as a gently reminder that even in the aftermath of life's most challenging moments, it is just like the phoenix.

The phoenix within

The legendary bird known as the Phoenix has long been seen as a representation of life's inherent cycle as well as the concepts of renewal and rebirth since it is revered throughout time and cultures. Its compelling narrative of rising from the ashes has offered peace to many people in their darkest hours, reminding us of the intrinsic strength of tenacity and the promise for rebirth that exists within each one of us. It has given solace to countless people.

The methodology of phoenix

The legend of the phoenix is so interwoven into the fabric of ancient mythology that it cannot be separated from it. The story may be found in Egyptian, Greek, and even Chinese stories; nevertheless, despite some minor differences from one culture to the next, the narrative always centers on the concept of life, death, and the miraculous reincarnation of the deceased.

Egyptian Origins

The Phoenix was also referred to as the Bennu bird when it lived in ancient Egypt. It was thought to represent the sun deity Ra's soul, and it was often shown as a heron with a large beak and a crown made of two feathers. According to folklore, the Bennu would construct a nest out of cinnamon twigs for itself once every five hundred years and then deliberately light it on fire. A youthful and strong new Bennu would emerge from the ashes of the burning Bennu, ready to begin a new life cycle.

Greek Adaptations

The Greeks gave the narrative its own unique twist when they adapted it. In this context, the image of the phoenix is that of a brilliant bird with golden and crimson plumage that is often associated with the sun. According to several legends, its lifespan might have ranged anywhere from 500 to 1000 years. When the time came for the phoenix to pass on, it would build a nest for itself out of fragrant branches and spices, and then set itself ablaze. The ashes would give birth to a new phoenix, which would be tasked with delivering a token from the previous bird to the temple of the sun at Heliopolis as a sign that the cycle of life would continue.

Chinese interpretations

According to traditional Chinese interpretations, the phoenix, also known as Feng Huang, was seen as a sign of elegance and morality in eastern cultures. In contrast to its equivalents in the West, it was not connected with being reborn via the use of fire. Instead, the sighting of it was seen as a portent of tranquility, signaling the start of a whole new age. The Feng Huang was the product of the marriage of masculine and female spirits, exemplifying the ideal of yin and yang coexisting in perfect harmony.

A Shining Example of Hope in These Contemporary Times

The persistent mystique of the phoenix is not relegated only to the stories of bygone eras. The symbolism of it has also been discovered to have relevance in more modern scenarios. Whether it is in a piece of writing, a movie, or just day-to-day life, the phoenix serves as a powerful reminder that even in the most trying of circumstances, fresh beginnings are still possible.

The story of the phoenix might provide a glimpse of hope to those who are going through difficult personal transitions such as divorce. Individuals, like the bird that rises from the ashes, may come out on the other side of their hardships, more resilient and experienced. This rebirth is not limited to the physical realm but also encompasses the emotional and spiritual dimensions.

The secret is in recognizing the suffering, gaining insight from the lessons it teaches, and using this newly acquired knowledge to pave the way for a future that is brighter and more satisfying. We, too, have the resiliency to confront hardship, to evolve, and to emerge from the ashes in a new shape, just like the phoenix.

Personal Stories of Rebirth after Divorce

Many people see divorce as the last chapter in their lives. However, for many people, it may also represent a chance to start again and find their own unique route in life. Divorce is a difficult experience, but it is also a chance to learn and develop as a person and go on with your life. These narratives will serve as living proof of this transforming potential. They exhibit the human capacity to bounce back from adversity and find meaning in life. These people from all areas of life have weathered the storm and come out on the other side more resilient, wiser, and full of life.

Sarah Takes a Flying Leap

Sarah had always been one to make detailed plans for her future. So, when her marriage of 15 years ended, everything she had worked so hard to create appeared to fall apart. That space was huge. Sarah, however, rejected this option in favor of taking the road less traveled. She packed her bags and uprooted to Italy for a year, completely immersing herself in the Italian language and culture. Sarah's love of art and history was reignited as she wandered the alleyways of Florence and the streets of Rome. At the conclusion of her vacation, she had not only rediscovered herself, but also developed a business strategy for a company that would provide customized tours of Italy. Sarah channeled her anguish into motivation by becoming a tour guide.

James' Unexpected Calling

The roles of husband and parent had always been central in James' identity. After his wife departed, he experienced profound grief and struggled to find his place in the world outside his family. James finally found peace of mind when he began mentoring elementary school students as a volunteer at his daughter's school. What began as chance meetings evolved into a professional vocation? He went on to complete his education and certification requirements to become a school counselor. James was able to heal his own scars and discover a greater meaning in life as a result of this experience.

Emma's Fateful Tango

Emma and her husband danced together and won several competitions and awards. Their dancing relationship dissolved when their marriage did. Emma was afraid to perform on the same stage where they had previously been so in tune. But instead of retiring from dancing, Emma set off on an adventure without anybody else. She tried on new looks that she never would have considered previously. All the dances helped, from classical to modern. Emma learned that sometimes you can create the most beautiful rhythms all on your own as her fresh solo act gave her worldwide attention.

Oliver's Eats and Exploits

Oliver took a major blow after his divorce. His wife and he had once dreamed of owning a café, but that idea had long since faded. One night when Oliver was thinking about things, he started baking, a hobby he hadn't done in years. The kitchen became his safe haven, and each meal he prepared had meaning for him. Friends urged Oliver to start throwing intimate dinner parties, which he did. As word of Oliver's meetings spread, the place became busier. The pain of loss that almost destroyed him ended up being the key to his culinary success.

Acknowledging your motions

Like any major life change, divorce may cause an emotional tsunami to wash over us. It has been quite a ride, with each day offering its own unique mix of emotions, trials, and introspections. More than just stamina is needed to make it through this emotional labyrinth; recognition is also essential. The road to recovery and development begins with self-awareness and emotional literacy. We may better confront these sensations head-on, process them, and ultimately find peace if we chart the normal phases individuals go through, from the raw pains of loss and the burning clutches of fury to the peaceful beaches of acceptance.

A Roadmap of Emotional Growth

Grief

A strong feeling of loss is common in the initial stages after a divorce. The finality of a relationship ending, even if the choice was mutual, may seem like the death of a loved one. Everything that was planned, everything that was remembered, it all stops. A time of sorrow is appropriate and healthy. It is an opportunity to take stock and mourn the loss of hope for the future that you and your spouse once had.

Grief is a complicated emotion, especially in its early stages after a divorce. Sadness, bewilderment, and even astonishment are all mixed together in one emotion. Many have compared the experience to that of stumbling about in the dark after emerging from a dense fog.

Sense of loss

Grief is driven by a profound awareness of loss. Losing someone is like losing a part of yourself, not simply a part of your everyday existence. Being a spouse, wife, or partner was foundational to many people's identities. Disorientation may set in when that function suddenly ceases to exist.

Remembering Together

Moments from the beginning of the relationship, whether they be the first date, an anniversary, or just a normal day, flood back. These once-happy recollections might now serve as painful reminders of what was previously held dear.

The End of Our Future Plans

Grief for a lost future is beyond the pain of remembering the past. All your shared hopes and ambitions — for the future of your home, your travels, or your old age — have been dashed.

It is crucial to give yourself plenty of time and room to mourn at this period. Suppressing or rushing the process may cause physical and mental health problems, as well as longer durations of discomfort.

Anger

When people finally accept the facts, they may get angry. Betrayal, frustration, and anger are among emotions that might emerge. It is normal to wonder what went wrong or to try to assign blame, either to yourself or to your spouse. Even though it hurts so much, this rage is a healthy aspect of recovery. Understanding, expressing (in constructive ways), and letting go of it are all crucial.

Anger typically takes its place when the haze of sadness starts to dissipate. It is a more proactive feeling that leaves behind a deceptive sensation of strength.

Searching for reasons

Anger typically results from a person's attempt to rationalize the breakup of a relationship. People try to assign blame, whether it is to their former spouse, external circumstances, or themselves.

Betrayal Sensations

Feelings of betrayal may compound resentment if the divorce was precipitated by adultery or any other violation of trust. When trust is betrayed, it produces emotional wounds that are particularly challenging to erase.

Venting Fury

It is important to find constructive ways to express your anger, even when such feelings are inevitable. The feeling may be processed and released via exercise, counseling, writing, or simply just chatting to a friend.

Acceptance

Emotional upheaval eventually gives way to acceptance because of time and insight. Just because you are at this stage does not imply you are "okay" or that the agony has totally subsided. Instead, it is a recognition of the present situation and a will to adapt. The first step toward a fresh start, self-discovery, and a world of new opportunities is accepting what is.

Coming to terms with something is a process that takes time and usually involves epiphanies along the way.

Realizing the Inevitability of Change

Realizing that change, no matter how difficult, is inevitable is the first step toward acceptance. It is about accepting that every part of your life has its own story arc, and that although some chapters end, others begin.

Regaining One's Identity

The freedom to explore oneself is a wonderful benefit of being accepted. Most people eventually come to terms with the fact that their identity is more than the sum of the relationships they have had. After years of marriage, they begin to rediscover individual passions and interests.

With an Eye on the Future

Future uncertainty decreases as resolve to accept grows. Individuals begin to take initiative, engage in goal-setting, and become more receptive to new contacts and experiences.

The healing process consists of a series of phases, each of which must be understood in order to be navigated effectively. When you learn and use the lessons and wisdom that come with each stage of life, you become more powerful and resilient.

Throughout this topic, we will go into further detail about each of these phases of emotion, providing insight, advice, and coping skills along the way. To reiterate, it is normal to experience emotion, pain, and recovery. Recognizing and accepting your feelings is a crucial first step toward a better future.

The Therapeutic Power of Understanding and Accepting Feelings

Major life changes, like a divorce, may trigger a roller coaster of emotions and leave a person feeling lost at sea. It is scary to try to make your way through this emotional hurricane. Understanding and embracing these feelings, though, may be helpful. Let us go into the depths of this idea and the revolutionary possibilities it presents.

Understanding Emotions: The Foundation of Recovery

Feeling Recognized

Every feeling — happiness, rage, sorrow, and even confusion — has a meaning. Feeling the feeling and learning to name it takes introspection and awareness of the self. Persistent melancholy, for instance, may point to unresolved bereavement, just as persistent anger may indicate unresolved conflict or emotions of betrayal.

Interpreting the Message

The next stage in decoding an emotion's message is figuring out why it is there in the first place. Why did that happen? Is it based on anything from your history, your present circumstances, or your future fears? Understanding the origin of an emotion helps one deal with it more successfully.

Reflection

Understanding emotions through contemplation, quiet introspection, and contemplation may be crucial. Understanding one's feelings requires introspection, and this may be achieved by journaling, meditation, or even just taking some time off to think.

The Key to Happiness Is Acknowledging Your Feelings

Zone de non-judgment

It is crucial to provide room in one's mind for feelings to exist without being evaluated. People's authentic emotions are often buried or denied conforming to society or personal expectations. Understanding that every feeling has a purpose allows one to deal with them without condemning themselves.

Emotions are fleeting

Feelings do not last forever since that's not how emotions work. They fluctuate, alter, and develop with time. Realizing that these feelings are fleeting will help alleviate the worry and panic that often accompany them. It is a helpful reminder that even the strongest emotions pass with time.

Seeking support

Accepting feelings may be difficult at times, particularly when they are all-consuming. The help of others, whether they be friends, family, or professionals, may be important at these times. Counselors and therapists may help you learn strategies for dealing with your feelings.

When you learn to recognize and embrace your feelings, you do more than simply survive; you thrive. By welcoming their feelings, people might find new pathways to self-improvement, closer relationships, and inner calm. It is like clearing off mental clutter to make room for exciting new adventures. Being in touch with and embracing one's emotions is a cornerstone of overall health and happiness.

Chapter 2

Empowerment through Knowledge and Support

Divorce is difficult not only emotionally, but also in terms of logistics and practicality. As you try to make sense of your emotions, you'll also have to deal with the exterior world of rules, choices, and relationships.

Let us work together to solve this problem. When you first start dealing with the legal aspects of a divorce, it might seem like you are attempting to read Chinese while walking a tightrope. Have faith; I understand. You may, however, find your way through this labyrinth with ease and confidence if you have access to the correct knowledge and a strong support system. This section? You may use it as both a light source and a navigational aid.

Navigating the Legal Maze

Breathe deeply for starters. I understand it; diving headfirst into the legal system without a life vest might be intimidating. On the other hand, did you know this? You have company. Together, we are going to simplify this to the point where a child could accomplish it. I am certain that with some direction and explanation, you will breeze through this. OK, so let us start:

Simplifying the legal proceedings

Do you recall the last time you attempted to put together one of those tricky pieces of furniture? You know, the one where you get a box of screws and some wood panels and no real directions on how to put it together? At first glance, you probably thought it was a mountain. That is right; I can relate. In the beginning, you may wonder, "Where do I even begin?"

Divorce proceedings are similar in that they might make you feel like you have opened that box all over again. You have been given a pile of paperwork with unfamiliar terminology that seems like they were plucked out from a Shakespearean play, and you are expected to grasp it all at once.

However, I will let you in on a little secret: there is a method behind the seeming chaos, just as there is with that furniture. Once you understand the fundamentals of how the legal system works, it will seem much less daunting.

Let us dispel some common misconceptions first.

Not all legal cases play out like epic courtroom confrontations between two equally matched opponents. With the correct attitude and comprehension, many legal procedures may be easy and friendly.

Do you recall how much more manageable it was to put up that furniture if you had a clear guide or a friend came over to help? This is exactly what we plan to accomplish. We will outline the major steps involved in the legal procedure, explain any unfamiliar terminology in simple English, and provide advice to help you along the way.

Remembering that there are trained specialists available to assist you in your time of need is also crucial. Despite appearances, lawyers are no more frightening than the customer service representatives you phone when you cannot figure out which screw fits where in your furniture. They have been there, done that, and can help you out.

Advocating for one's rights

Now we have arrived at a critical juncture: speaking out for yourself. It's like the moment in every hero film when the main character finally stands up for themselves. And now it is your turn to shine, just as it was for them.

The reluctance is very understandable to me. The apprehension of offending others or the anxiety of finding one's way through the maze of regulations. Here is another way I will say it: Let us pretend you are at a crowded café, and you have just ordered a coffee. After a little time, a cup of tea is brought to you. You did not ask for tea, did you? Would you please take it discreetly and gulp it down? Or you might highlight the mix-up and ask for your correct order.

The law protects you in much the same way. It is not about making a fuss or seeking the spotlight, but rather about getting what is rightly yours. Similarly, to the café example, there is a method to accomplish it without losing your composure.

To begin, there is a significant gap between assertiveness and aggression that must be bridged. Whereas assertiveness creates channels of communication, aggressiveness may shut them off. Respecting people and making sure they respect you are fundamental to this.

Studying the law and arguing for your rights involves some preparation. In this setting, knowledge really is power. Learn what benefits you are entitled to. The more prepared you are for a topic, the more at ease you will feel participating in it.

The key to success is reliable communication. It is like carrying around a multi tool with all the blades out. Clarity, composure, and asking clarifying questions are the hallmarks of effective communication, not shouting. It is OK to ask for clarification numerous times until you fully understand. After all, you must live your own life.

Finally, keep in mind that you have support from others. There are others out there who have gone through the same thing as you, including lawyers, support groups, and even friends. Depend on them. Talk it out and get some input on your problems. They can provide insights you had not thought about before.

You should be able to carry your head high down this road because you are taking care of yourself and standing up for what you deserve. Have faith in yourself and your abilities. And keep in mind that standing up for yourself today will serve as a model for any future actions you conduct. I believe in you and will be rooting for you the whole way through this challenge.

Building a Support System

Here we are, discussing the priceless basis of a solid support system, an issue near and dear to my heart and, I think, to everyone. It is analogous to a building's foundation, a tree's roots, or the unseen threads that bind a quilt's squares together. The strength, balance, and coherence it provides may not always be obvious, but it is always there.

The ups and downs of life often present us with unanticipated obstacles. In addition to the unquestionable force of individual resilience, the power of communal resilience cannot be overstated. In times of self-doubt, when the way ahead is unclear, or when we just need to vent, our support system shines like a lighthouse.

The value of family, friends, and support groups

Remember how satisfying it is when all the parts of a puzzle, LEGO structure, or that piece of furniture you are putting together go together like they were meant to all work together? The great and at times difficult turns of life also function in this manner. The people closest to us, our support system, are invaluable, especially during trying times like a divorce.

Let us say you're day hiking. There is some validity to going at it alone. But consider how much more enjoyable, reassuring, and memorable the experience is with a friend or a group. When the going gets tough, they will provide a hand, and when you are feeling puckish, they will split a snack with you.

That is the power of having people behind you.

Family

The traditional social network of a person's family. In many ways, families may be compared to a multi-purpose tool. They have seen you at your finest, lowest, and all points in between. They have shared every emotion with you: laughter, sadness, and silence. Despite the fact that families have a wide range of structures, we often find stability among our closest relationships. It is important to have somebody in our lives who we can talk to about the difficulties of life, whether it is a sibling to complain to, a parent to provide advice, or a cousin to make the finest jokes.

Friends

Are you familiar with the adage, "Friends are the family we choose?" So much of it is true. Friends are the people you have chosen for yourself based on your similar interests, values, and experiences. They are the people you turn to when you need an unexpected night out, someone to weep on, or sound advice. They may provide a new viewpoint during challenging times, or they might just listen without passing judgment. All of our friends enrich our lives in their own special ways.

Support groups

Sometimes we just need a place to go where other people "get it." In cases like this, community groups excel. They are a group of people bound together by shared experiences, struggles, and sentiments. A listening ear and an experienced person's perspective may be found in places like internet discussion boards, community center groups, and therapeutic circles. Knowing you are not alone on your path and hearing others' experiences may be quite empowering.

Constant effort is required to build and maintain a strong network of allies. Recognizing who supports you, establishing limits with those who do not, and reaching out to new people, when necessary, all play a part. Keep in mind that you can rely on other people just as much as they can rely on you. After all, we are all in this thing called life together, and we need each other's strength and encouragement to get it through.

Consider the people who are there for you right now. Treat them with respect and gratitude, and rest certain that with them at your side, you can take on anything.

Recognizing and avoiding toxic relationships

Finding one's way through the complex web of interpersonal interactions might seem like navigating a maze. There is something valuable and instructive to be learned from every single relationship. While many of these elements strengthen the tapestry of our lives, others might weaken it. This is what most of us mean when we talk about "toxic relationships."

Relationship Toxicology

A toxic relationship is characterized by a steady drain on emotional reserves and a gradual erosion of self-esteem. It is characterized by cycles of destructive behavior, power plays, and disharmony. Partners, friends, relatives, and even coworkers may all count. Recognizing the signals is the first step in navigating these seas. Be wary of somebody who seems to be experiencing persistent emotions of worry, poor self-esteem, or awkwardness with others. These are typical warning signs that something is wrong.

Things to Keep an Eye On

- **Constant criticism**
Constant criticism, on the other hand, is not constructive and should be avoided. Someone in your life who is often finding fault

with or putting down your accomplishments should raise warning flags.

- **Manipulative behavior**

This might be overt, like making threats or giving you an ultimatum, or covert, like using a guilt trip. Learn to identify situations in which another person is attempting to manipulate your behavior or feelings for their own benefit.

- **Undefined Boundaries**

The demand for privacy and the recognition of other people's limits is universal. A toxic dynamic exists when one person repeatedly violates your personal space or shows little concern for your emotions.

Actions to Take for Survival

The first step in improving your mental health is becoming aware of the challenges you face. Clearly state what you will and will not tolerate and stick to those limits. Maintaining these limits may be difficult, but it is essential.

- **Count on Dependable Friends and Family**

Telling a trusted friend or family member about your worries might help you see things more clearly.

- **Put Your Health First**

Never forget to prioritize yourself first. This is not egocentric; rather, it is necessary. Rest, think, and believe in yourself again.

If you feel like you cannot manage the problem on your own, do not be afraid to seek professional help. Consulting an expert may provide you with the resources you need to manage these kinds of partnerships.

You have the right to make your relationships satisfying and pleasant even when they are intricate and multifaceted. Learn from your mistakes and remember that you are worthy of having relationships that appreciate and honor who you are. Here is to fostering connections based on trust and admiration!

Chapter 3

The Path to Self-Care

Hello there, beautiful being! You have entered a period of your life that will change you in profound ways. Moving on after a divorce, it is important to keep in mind that even if external circumstances may be less than ideal, the core of your being is as strong and beautiful as ever. The moment is now to focus within, to nourish and adore that amazing soul of yours. Believe me, this has nothing to do with putting oneself first; rather, it is about starting again and reigniting the spark inside.

Nurture your soul

After experiencing a major life upheaval, such as a divorce, it is common to feel emotionally and physically fatigued as a result of the aftereffects. However, much like a garden, our spirit thrives with little TLC. Self-care after divorce is more than a passing fad; it is a vital link between your current situation and the future you want for yourself. It is about establishing solid habits that provide comprehensive nourishment for your body and mind.

Reconnecting with oneself is the ultimate goal of activities like morning yoga, quiet time in nature, or even that overdue trip to the spa.

Like our physical body, our spiritual self needs regular attention. This kind of care is not optional, but rather essential, particularly during times of change. We need to make sure our soul feels loved, appreciated, and valued if we want to recover, regain our enthusiasm, and go ahead with optimism.

The importance of self-care post-divorce

Divorce involves more than simply the formalities of the law. It involves the heart, the head, and the soul. The feelings are genuine and may be intense. This is when tender care comes in handy. When we put ourselves first, we create a sanctuary where our spirit may mend, reflect, and develop.

Whether the split is amicable or contentious, it will have a profound impact on both parties. It is more than simply a breakup or a property settlement; it is a profound emotional shift that resets your entire world. You may feel that you are being overlooked in the thick of court processes, debates over who should get what, and restless evenings spent trying to figure out what went wrong.

Self-care is more important than ever before. What is the reason you inquire? Now, let us dissect this into its component parts.

Repairing Emotional Hurts

The emotional ups and downs experienced after a divorce are often overwhelming. Sadness, then rage, then maybe even relief follow one another. Damage may be incurred in this whirlwind. By giving the soul the time and space, it needs to recover, self-care functions as a balm on fresh emotional wounds.

Recognizing One's Own Value

Doubts about one's value are prevalent after a divorce. "Was it my fault?" "Could I have done something different?" Taking care of yourself is an act of self-love. It is a symbol of my appreciation for you, single or married.

Condition of the Body

Divorce stress may lead to actual bodily symptoms. A person's health might be negatively impacted by factors such as lack of sleep, poor diet, or stress. Self-care is the practice of giving one's own body the care and rest that it needs and deserves.

Strengthening Resilience

There are highs and lows in everyone's lives. If you take care of yourself, you will be more prepared to deal with challenges. It teaches people to persevere through adversity.

Preparing the Ground for Future Connections

You are an example to others if you know and value yourself. You know what you want and need in future relationships, whether they are platonic or romantic, and you have a firm grasp on the limits that are necessary to protect yourself.

Reestablishing a Personal Connection

It is easy to lose track of who we are as individuals in the twirl of romantic partnerships. Self-care after divorce enables you to find and appreciate your individuality as you enter a new phase of life.

In essence, self-care after a divorce entails more than simply visits to the spa or a relaxing getaway. It is a trip within oneself, a reconnecting with one's own identity. It is realizing that even in the middle of change and uncertainty, you are the one constant. When you take care of yourself, you do more than simply get back up; you take steps toward a better future.

Holistic approaches to physical and mental well-being

In the wake of a divorce, it is important to see our health as a whole, including both our physical and emotional aspects. The wonderful thing about holistic health is that it does not isolate any one part of you but rather considers you as a whole. And, truth be told, this all-encompassing approach is exactly what we need to recover with vigor and grace after a life-altering catastrophe like a divorce.

The Unity of Body and Mind

For starters, let us debunk a widespread misconception: physical and mental health are not two independent states but rather, two sides of the same coin. When our bodies feel good, our spirits tend to rise, and when our minds are at peace and filled with optimism, our bodies tend to respond by being more energized and vibrant.

Food is more than simply fuel

It nourishes the body and the spirit. It is a treatment. It is soothing. A token of affection. Eating complete, nutritious meals has far-reaching effects on our mental and emotional health, in addition to the obvious physical benefits. To improve your body and mind, try eating more colorful vegetables, healthy grains, and fish high in omega-3 fatty acids.

Physical activity

Physical activity may serve as a kind of meditation, and the benefits can be immense. These actions not only strengthen muscles and burn calories, but also trigger the release of endorphins, the body's natural feel-good chemicals. Also, like meditation, the act of concentrating on movement provides a welcome reprieve from the constant stream of ideas.

Mindfulness practices

Make an effort to include mindfulness practices like meditation in your daily routine. These methods teach us to focus on the here and now, bringing peace even in the face of difficulty. It is like taking a vacation for your brain.

Sleep

A good night's sleep may do wonders for your body and mind. It is when your mental and physical faculties have a chance to recharge and mend. Maintaining a sleep schedule of 7 to 9 hours every night has been shown to significantly improve cognitive performance, psychological fortitude, and vitality.

Natural Medications

Sometimes it is better to go back to basics. You may find solace from your body's aches and calm your mind with the help of meditation, prayer, acupuncture, aromatherapy, and other alternative therapies.

Humans thrive in group settings that foster interaction and mutual support. The emotional support and fleeting moments of delight provided by participating in community activities, joining support groups, or even simply maintaining close personal relationships may be like a salve for the soul.

Keep in mind that attaining holistic wellness is a very individual process. What strikes a chord with one person may not do so with another. The important thing is to try new things out until you discover what works best for you. Imagine these holistic methods as tools in your toolbox that will aid in your rebuilding, rejuvenation, and rekindling of your inner beauty as you commit to them. After all, you are doing more than merely surviving in the wake of your divorce. This complete method will help you achieve your goals with grace and style.

Rediscovering Your Passions

Do you long for the days when you could immerse yourself in an enjoyable book, a dance, or a painting? Remember how sometimes time would fly by in the blink of an eye and everything else would fade into the background? Those were the moments when you were totally immersed in what really inspired you.

The many demands of daily life might make it difficult to prioritize things like hobbies and interests. As life-altering and difficult as experiences like divorce might be, they frequently hasten our drift away from the things that formerly gave us inexpressible delight. But here is some advice: old love can always be reignited, and new passions may always be ignited.

Revisiting old hobbies and discovering new ones

Sometimes, life has a funny way of becoming busy and putting our favorite pastimes to the sidelines. We already struggle with change and emotions through major changes like getting a divorce, which further pushes these interests to the background. But it is also a fantastic opportunity to reconnect with yourself and the world by exploring new interests or revisiting old ones.

The Importance of Hobbies

An individual's hobby is more than simply something they do in their spare time. They help us understand ourselves, provide us with direction, and comfort us through challenging times. One of the many benefits of taking up a pastime is the mental and emotional respite it may provide.

Encourage original thought by exposing your brain to fresh experiences.

Increase Your Confidence:
- Creating a feeling of fulfillment.

The Longing for Past Interests:
- Resuming an old interest is a lot like reconnecting with a long-lost friend.

Boost self esteem
- It brings up pleasant memories and is so soothing.

Nostalgia of hobbies

Hobbies may be a gateway back to a more carefree era. If you want to relive your glory days of adolescence singing with your friends, all you have to do is pick up an old guitar.

Having previously pursued a pastime gives you a head start on the path to mastery. This moment might be ideal for mastering those abilities to their full potential.

Finding Uncharted Ground
The delight of discovering a new interest is comparable to the excitement of rekindling an old one. There are many experiences out there just waiting to be had.

Expanding One's Perspectives
Trying out a new pastime is like walking through an unknown door. Learning a new hobby or activity, such as pottery, trekking, or digital photography, may help you see the world in a different light.

Establishing New Contacts
Most times when you take up a new hobby, you end up meeting people from all around. You may meet new individuals with similar interests by signing up for a dancing class or a reading club.

Perfect blend
Striking a balance is essential as you travel this journey of rediscovery. Even while it is exciting to start a new hobby, returning to an old one may be a nostalgic experience.

Making a Weekly Schedule
Dedicate some days to both long-standing interests and promising new pursuits. This guarantees that you get the highest quality of both worlds.

The Importance of Goal-Setting

Setting concrete objectives gives your efforts, whether they be learning a difficult guitar piece or completing a difficult hike, more meaning.

Creating pockets of happiness in the new phase of life

The only constant in life is change. The aftermath of a divorce, for example, may throw lengthy, often gloomy shadows, making even the brightest days seem drab. But it is feasible, and perhaps essential, to identify and cultivate oases of joy among all this change. Tiny bursts of happiness like this might serve as guiding lights for the future.

The Science of Contentment

Being happy is more than simply a feeling; it is a way of life. It is crucial to keep in mind that joy does not necessarily entail being completely free of sorrow. Happiness is a feeling that can live alongside others, and it serves as a subtle reminder of the beauty that exists among the complexities of life.

Persona definition

How happy you are is quite individual. What makes one person happy may not make another person happy at all. Having a clear idea of what makes you happy is essential.

Developing a Routine

Mindfulness applied to ordinary activities may unlock hidden wells of happiness.

Early Reflections
Get your day off to a good start. This might be anything from meditating for a few minutes to taking in the morning sky with a cup of coffee. The tone for the day is established by these customs.

Record your Gratitude
Write down three things for which you are thankful every night before bed. It helps you concentrate less on the things that are lacking in your life and more on the many things that are working well.

Retrieved Area

Our mental health is profoundly influenced by the environments we live in. After a divorce, these places may trigger painful flashbacks. Reclaiming and redefining them is crucial.

Redecorate
The smallest of shifts might result in a surge of renewed enthusiasm. Move things about, get some new pillows, and maybe even paint a wall your favorite color.

A Place of Safety

Set aside some personal space in your house. It might be a place to relax and read, grow some plants, or work on a hobby. You may use this area as a place to relax and recharge.

Social Connections

Humans need meaningful relationships with others in order to flourish. Maintaining long-standing friendships is important, but making new connections is as so.

Participate in Local Events

Participate in community gatherings, classes, and organizations. They provide venues for interacting with new individuals and developing connections.

Volunteer

Making other people happy is a certain way to find your own. It is fulfilling to know you are making a difference in people's lives.

Self-Care as a Priority

Well-being and contentment go hand in hand.

Condition of the body

Enjoy yourself by doing things like yoga, dancing, or just going on long walks.

Psychological Health

Try meditation, counseling, or just deep breathing techniques to help you relax and unwind.

There is beauty in the ups and downs of this journey we call life. In this next phase of your life, it will be important to actively seek out and cultivate moments of joy. They become the anchors you hold on to, the beams of light that show you that the human spirit is strong and beautiful. Honor them, keep them close, and they will lead you to a happy, successful life.

Chapter 4

Parenting and Transition

Divorce is already difficult enough without adding the responsibility of raising children into the mix. We adults have our own emotional waves to weather, and in the midst of them, it may be easy to lose sight of the fact that our children are experiencing their own storms of uncertainty, loss, and transformation.

This section is for the many parents who are working hard to keep their kids stable, loved, and comprehended despite the chaos around them. It is a process that begins with recognizing the unseen challenges our kids face, continues with giving them the tools they need to overcome adversity, and culminates in establishing a cooperative parenting arrangement that prioritizes the kids' happiness.

While every family's experiences are unique, there are common threads that might help us along the way. All families go through difficulties, but children need to know that their parents' love for them is constant, unconditional, and ever-expanding no matter what.

In the next chapters, we will talk at length about the psychological support kids need from their parents after a divorce, how to co-parent successfully, and how to teach resilience to the next generation. Keep in mind that our response to a challenging circumstance is what our kids will remember most. Let us start this trip together, with kindness, intelligence, and faith in a better future for our children.

Transition through parenting

Divorce is just one example of the many life changes that may bring their own unique set of difficulties. This holds truer than ever when young people are engaged. A profound change in the family dynamic might be unsettling for a child whose worldview is still developing.

Realizing Their Perspective

Children have a remarkable capacity for insight. They are sensitive to the atmosphere and may sense tension or emotion before words are spoken. To help them adjust, you must first recognize the environment in which they operate. Everything they are accustomed to, from their daily routines to the consistency of their lives to the precious small moments they have with their parents must shift. And although it may take adults some time to come to terms with the prospect of a divorce, the children are often thrown into the aftermath unprepared.

Connecting with One Another

Although it may seem cliche, open communication is of paramount significance. Children are naturally curious and naturally fearful. It is crucial to foster an atmosphere where people may freely express their opinions without fear of repercussion. Do not sugarcoat the truth while answering their queries; just keep their ages and maturity levels in mind. They do not need to know everything, but they should know what is going on.

Regularity and Predictability

The stability of routine may be a haven in turbulent times. Maintain as much regularity as you can throughout their daily schedule. Keeping to the same bedtime story, school schedule, or weekend activities is one way to do this. These recurring habits may provide solace and stability among all the upheavals.

Consensus in Parenting

Quality time with both parents is more important than quantity of time spent with either. If kids can see their parents working together and talking constructively, it will help the transition go more smoothly for them. It is important to put up a unified face and keep any arguments out of the children's eyes.

Developing New Recollections

It is also a terrific opportunity to start brand-new customs and traditions. Perhaps it is a change to the way you say good night, the frequency of your outings, or the way you mark important life events. Even while it is important to teach children that change may bring them wonderful new beginnings; it is also important to show them that consistency via routines is key.

Transitional parenting is really about striking a balance between comforting your child with familiarity and encouraging them to embrace change, acknowledging their anxieties and helping them overcome them, and so on. Parenting is an adventure in which you and your child will both learn and develop.

The emotional and psychological needs of children during divorce

When a couple's lives are turned upside down by the upheaval of a divorce, it is easy for the parents to lose sight of the inborn emotional and psychological need of their children for safety and stability.

In the event that you and your spouse decide to divorce, you should always prioritize the needs of your children before your own requirements. There are people in this world who will tell you that if you do not take care of your own needs, you are not going to be able to meet the needs of your kid. They say this because they believe it to be true. I would argue against the validity of this notion. After working with a large number of families who have been through the process of divorce, I can tell you that there are very few people who are completely willing to neglect their own needs and position their case in a way that is beneficial to their children to the greatest extent possible. With that being said, there is always room for each of us to be more generous and considerate of the requirements of the people in our lives. If it is clear to everyone that you are going through a divorce, the requirements of your kid should take precedence over anything else.

Divorce is a fact of life, and one of those facts is that it always results in change, and that change may be incredibly significant for families. Regardless of how settled you believe your family to be despite the divorce, I can nearly guarantee that you will be confronted with a number of challenges as a direct consequence of having gone through the process of getting a divorce. Some of these alterations will be beneficial to the situation, while others will not be. Some of these shifts are ones that you can anticipate, while others will sneak up on you like a freight train out of nowhere and knock you off your feet. Some people believe that change is inevitable, yet there are times when we wish that evolution would speed faster so that we could catch up.

The positive aspect of going through a divorce as an adult is that you have some frame of reference that life will reach a point of normality in the future and that you will be able to adapt to the changes that have taken place in your life. This is an advantage that you do not have while going through a divorce as a child. You will reach a moment in your life when things begin to slow down, and you will begin to establish a rhythm once again. This point will arrive at a time when you believe the changes will never end. If you were to ask a person going through a divorce what they want, I can always guarantee that they would tell you that the changes they are experiencing are ones that they want to slow down and allow them to catch their breath. This is despite the fact that we all seek change in our day-to-day lives.

People who are contemplating getting a divorce are encouraged by me to give this particular point of view some serious thought before making their final decision. To be more specific, of all the things that you are fed up with and upset with about your marriage, family life, and everything in between, what percentage of those frustrations are attributable to you and things that you have control over, and what percentage of those frustrations are attributable to the fact that you are married to your current partner? If a considerable number of the adjustments that you feel are required can be brought about only by you, then you probably do not need a divorce after all. It is true that getting a divorce is simpler than it has ever been in the history of our nation, but the fact of the matter is that there are instances when the divorce that you want is not in your best interest or the best interest of your family.

The truth about divorce is that many of the changes we want are ones that we can bring about in our own lives without having to go through the challenges and heartache that come along with the dissolution of a marriage. However, in order to arrive at that conclusion, you need to look at yourself with a critical eye and be harsh on yourself based on your inadequacies, selfish inclinations, myopic criticisms of your spouse, and other personality flaws that we all have. This may come across as harsh language, and believe me when I say that I am also guilty of these characteristics myself; however, in order to be honest with ourselves, we need to be able to take a somewhat stern look that's where we fall short in our marriages, and then work together with their spouses to remedy those problems to the extent that we are able.

The psychological and emotional needs of your child may vary with their age.

When it comes to their feelings, adolescents are in a difficult place, as can be attested to by everyone who has ever coached a team in which their children participated. When we look at a teenager, we can perceive a child who is slowly maturing into an adult. Teenagers are more grown physically than children are, and they begin to take on features of adults in their mannerisms, physique, and general way of conducting themselves. Teenagers are more mature than toddlers. It is possible that, depending on how mature your adolescent is, you may easily forget that they are still a kid after all. However, below the mature-appearing attitude is a brain that is not yet completely matured, which is something that has to be taken into consideration while going through the process of getting a divorce.

Teenagers may be less likely to blame themselves for their parents' divorce, but they may be more willing to cast the responsibility for the divorce on one parent over the other. Teenagers, like most of the rest of us, are quick to pass judgment and are often more eager to claim that either the mother or the father is to blame for the collapse of the marriage, placing the responsibility for the dissolution of the marriage on that parent's shoulders. This puts you in a challenging situation as a parent since it is probable that your kid has a restricted picture of the facts surrounding your case, and on top of that, your child is not ready or able to examine the whole of the conditions that you have gone through. This places you in a tough position.

In the case of adolescents, it is necessary to have conversations with them on an adult level about the aspects of divorce that are relevant to them. It is not necessary for you to speak in a childlike manner to your adolescent or to dumb down the words that you use. Teenagers will value the fact that you treat them like adults and speak to them in an authoritative manner while maintaining a kind attitude. Your adolescent child is aware that, despite the fact that they may seem to be yearning for their independence on the surface, they are still dependent upon the guidance and direction that they get from you. If you are aware of how the divorce process works and what the most probable timeframe is, you will be able to offer your kid stability and consistency throughout this time.

The requirements of children of school age from an emotional and psychological standpoint

If you are the parent of children who are still in elementary or middle school but have not yet reached their teenage years, then your children are more likely to blame themselves for the divorce than the other parent. Children of this age have a tendency to see the world through the lens of themselves as the center of the universe, which is a limited perspective. This is a kind of narcissism that we as adults have ideally learnt to put aside as adults, but children at that age are not capable of doing so. As a consequence of this, the dissolution of your marriage must be in some way directly related to them. This creates a significant amount of pressure on relationships and a significant amount of mental strain on the brains of children who are of school age.

Assuring your children who are of school age that the dissolution of your marriage was not caused by them in any way is a greatly beneficial thing that you can do for them. Children of school age are not yet able to appreciate the difficulties associated with a troubled marriage; nonetheless, you may reassure them that both of their parents still love them and that this love will not alter no matter what the outcome of the divorce may be. You are also able to advise your kid by sharing with them information on the ways in which you will continue to put them at the center of your life despite the fact that other things are occurring. The last piece of this would be to make sure that, when you are going through a divorce, you always take the time to spend with your school-aged children in order to maintain and build your ties with them. This will help keep things stable throughout the divorce.

Preschoolers' emotional and psychological needs

Do not, under any circumstances, minimize the effect that a divorce will have on your children who are too young to attend school. The fact that these youngsters may not be able to read yet does not indicate that your children are unable to read you and understand your emotions very well. It is quite likely that these children have never ever heard the term "divorce," much less know what it means. Having said that, they will immediately notice the changes that you and your family are going through, the most notable difference being that your mother and father are no longer living together. Your children could have trouble adjusting to this, especially if they are used to having both of their parents present at the house.

Even while there is no alternative for both parents being present in the house, you and your partner may make an effort to spend as much time together as possible and divide up the responsibilities of parenting. Children of preschool age cannot have in-depth conversations regarding the impending divorce; nonetheless, it is extremely ideal to continually reinforce your affection for one another via physical exercise. The emotional and psychological requirements of your kid who has not yet reached the age of schooling are intimately related to the physical acts of love that you provide for them. No matter the outcome of the divorce, your preschool-aged children will be in a better position if you are able to continue showing them attention, being physically present with them, and having enthusiasm for them.

Care for the Young and Heart

Everyone engaged in a divorce goes through emotional upheaval, but it is especially important to keep in mind that the children are frequently the ones who take the worst hit. We must keep their emotions and requirements at the forefront of our thoughts as we go forward.

A Place of Freedom of Expression

Children, like adults, need a secure environment in which to share their feelings. Inspire them to share their experiences and validate their feelings. Reassure them that it is all right to feel and express whatever it is they are experiencing, whether it is grief, perplexity, or rage.

Regularity and Stability

Young people benefit much from regularity. It is crucial that they keep their routines consistent despite the turmoil of their divorce. Regular meals, lights out, and school attendance are all examples of this. Having things go as planned might make people feel at ease.

Affectionate and Comforting Words

Children of divorce can experience increased emotions of insecurity and abandonment. Assure them that their parents still care passionately for them even when they are going through a divorce. Give them plenty of hugs and kisses and do anything you can to make them feel special and appreciated.

Free and frank exchange of ideas

Young ones need explanations. Give them an age-appropriate explanation of what is going on, stressing that it was not their fault and that both parents will still be involved in their lives. Respond honestly and reassuringly to their inquiries.

Avoid or Reduce Conflict

Children might suffer tremendous emotional pain when their parents are constantly fighting. It is important to have an amicable co-parenting relationship and keep disagreements out of the kids' presence. One effective means of satisfying their emotional need is to keep them safe from harm.

Help from Experts, if Necessary

It may be necessary in certain situations to seek professional help for a youngster. Counselors or therapists with expertise in child psychology may assist children in understanding and managing their emotions. If you think your kid is having trouble adjusting, do not wait to get them assistance.

To Promote Positive Expression

Model appropriate methods of expressing feelings for youngsters. Creating something, keeping a diary, or going for a run are all examples of this. In the middle of the turmoil, these channels may help people deal with their emotions and regain some sense of control.

It takes patience, empathy, and a profound commitment to the well-being of the children to address their emotional needs throughout a divorce. It is not an easy path, but with our support, they will be able to take it in stride and emerge stronger on the other side.

Strategies for effective co-parenting

Co-parenting after a divorce is a delicate ballet, and like any sophisticated performance, it demands practice, patience, and a shared vision of harmony. While it is no question a tough trip, it can also be a route toward development, understanding, and the fostering of your children's well-being. Here, we dig into ways to assist you traverse this road with grace and effectiveness:

Prioritize Communication

Effective co-parenting is built on open lines of communication. It is not just about sharing logistics; it is about understanding, collaboration, and mutual respect. Establish a communication strategy that works for both of you, ensuring you keep updated about your children's needs, schedules, and any big events in their lives. Keep talks focused on your children's best interests and avoid wandering into personal problems.

Create a Detailed Parenting Plan

A well-structured parenting plan is like a blueprint that guides your co-parenting journey. It should be comprehensive, encompassing everything from visiting schedules to holiday arrangements, decision-making procedures affecting your children's education and healthcare, and even methods for dispute resolution. A clear strategy avoids misunderstanding and gives a foundation for collaboration.

Be Flexible and Cooperative

Flexibility is a feature of excellent co-parenting. Life is unpredictable, and events may emerge that demand revisions to your parenting plan. Accept these shifts as inevitable and collaborate to develop answers that serve your children's best interests. Your willingness to bend and work together is a reflection of how much you value your children.

Uniformity among Families

Children benefit from stability when there is no change in the rules, discipline, or expectations across homes. While it is only normal for each parent to have their own parenting style, it is important to talk about and agree on important matters like bedtime rituals, screen time restrictions, and punishments for disobedience so that your children know the ground rules in both households.

Honor one another's responsibilities

Your parental responsibilities have not changed because of the divorce. Be respectful of one other's choices and approaches to parenting. Keep unpleasant comments about each other out of the children's earshot and do not undermine each other's authority in front of them. Children are stronger when they stand together, and they should never feel pressured to choose a side.

Keep Kids Away from Fighting

Keep your differences with your co-parent from affecting your children. Do not bring up arguments or unpleasant feelings while they are around. You should never have a child choose sides in an argument or make them feel responsible for resolving it. Give them a place to vent their emotions without fear of repercussions.

Be thoughtful about transitions
Children often struggle during the transition between homes. Prepare carefully for these transitions. Keep the peace and routine by making sure your kids are prepared for their time with the other parent. They may feel better after hearing your words of comfort.

Get some help via mediation or therapy
Get professional assistance from a mediator or counselor who specializes in co-parenting challenges if arguments keep flaring up and solutions to problems remain elusive. A third person may act as a guide, encourage productive dialogue, and lead you to areas of agreement.

Promote Time Spent Together
Both parents need to make an effort to spend quality time alone with their kids. Children get a feeling of safety and affection from their parents via these interactions. Promote actions that let both parents spend one-on-one time with their kids.

Self-Care

Finally, take care of yourself first and foremost if you want to be a good co-parent. It is critical to prioritize one's own mental and physical health. A parent who is well and content is in a better position to provide their kids with the love and stability they need.

As with any journey, co-parenting successfully may have its difficulties. It requires a mutual dedication to your children's pleasure and well-being, as well as patience and sensitivity. You may help your children flourish and develop in a loving atmosphere after your divorce if you and your ex-spouse work together and always maintain your attention on them.

Building resilience in children

The effects of a parent's divorce on their children may be devastating. They need our love and support as they go through this change, but we also need to teach them the skills they will need to persevere. Children who develop resilience are better able to deal with setbacks, embrace change, and go on with confidence. Here are some ways to help your kids become more resilient:

Communicate freely and truthfully

Discuss divorce with your kids openly and honestly at their developmental stages. Allow children to share their opinions and emotions without fear of being labeled. Just tell them the truth and comfort them that they did nothing wrong. Please reassure them that both of their parents care strongly about them and want to be active in their lives.

Be there for them emotionally

Make your home a warm and accepting place where your kids can be themselves. Help children understand that negative emotions like sadness, anger, and confusion are normal human experiences. Be present to reassure them and acknowledge their feelings.

Be consistent

Children benefit from stability and security brought forth by regular, predictable routines and expectations. It is best if the two houses could maintain some degree of uniformity in terms of routines, norms, and schedules. Children may feel more at ease when things are consistent.

Inspire Creative Problem-Solving

Make age-appropriate choices together with your kids. They gain self-assurance and a feeling of mastery as a result. Motivate them to think creatively about how to solve problems.

Promote Flexibility

Divorce is only one of the many transitions that people go through throughout their lifetimes. Instill in your kids a willingness to adapt by showing them how change can be a positive experience. Be an example of resiliency through how you deal with adversity.

Relationships that lift you up

You should stress the importance of your children keeping close ties with their extended family, friends, and teachers. These ties provide new dimensions to one's network of care and affection.

Learn to Deal with Stress

Raise resilient young adults by teaching them effective techniques for managing stress and intense emotions. Some examples of these methods include meditation, writing in a diary, or doing something creative.

Aim Reasonably

Instruct your kids to aim for, and make progress toward, their objectives. They may gain confidence and fortitude from even the smallest of victories.

Self-Care Advocacy

Teach your kids the value of taking care of themselves by encouraging healthy habits like eating, sleeping, and moving around. Maintaining mental and physical wellness goes hand in hand.

Children's resilience must be built over time. It calls for calmness, sympathy, and dedication to their happiness. You can help your kids overcome the difficulties of your divorce and develop into strong, capable adults if you provide them with the resources they need.

Chapter 5

Reclaiming and Evolving

It is common for people to reevaluate their identities and their goals after going through a divorce. In this section, we set out on a quest for self-discovery, asking how one might find their own unique sense of self when the constraints of marriage have been removed.

Marriage, for many people, comes to represent an essential part of who they are. Divorce may make you feel as if a vital part of yourself has been severed. The exciting thing is that divorce provides a chance to start again and rediscover parts of yourself that may have been buried under the role of spouse. We will talk about techniques for getting to the core of who you are, the person who has been there the whole time but has been waiting for the proper opportunity to shine through.

Inspiring accounts of people who have overcome the difficulties of divorce to become better, more self-reliant people may be found throughout this chapter. These inspiring accounts of individual development serve as reminders that even in the darkest of circumstances, there is the possibility for great progress and self-discovery.

Divorce is a traumatic experience, but mindfulness may help you heal and develop in the aftermath. We will investigate exercises and methods that might help you develop mindfulness in your everyday life. You will learn to center yourself in the here and now via techniques including meditation, deep breathing, and self-compassion exercises.

Divorce may be an emotional roller coaster that makes you both nostalgic and fearful of the future. But the present moment is when healing and development really happen. We will go into the practice of being present in the "now," cultivating an attitude of thankfulness for one's current situation and building on it as a means of self-improvement.

Reclaiming Your Identity

The very core of who you are may be upended by a divorce. Your previous identity as a husband has been shattered, and you find yourself wondering, "Who am I now?" Here, we will go out on a quest for personal growth and learn how to remake ourselves after marriage.

Defining oneself beyond the confines of marriage

Marriage is a major milestone in most people's lives. The relationship determines how we spend our time each day, what we choose to do, and even how we feel about ourselves. Loss of one's marriage and the identity associated with it is a frequent emotion for those going through a divorce. You may have to reevaluate the parts you played, the sacrifices you made, and the goals you formerly held in common.

Marriage's Enormous Impact on Society

Marriage is a major part of the fabric of most people's lives. Over time, this position might consume one's whole life. As a result of this partnership, you may have adjusted to the roles of partner, husband, and even parent. Daily rituals, joint obligations, and the gradual blending of separate personalities into a unified whole characterize this stage.

Yet when divorce enters the scene, it might seem as if your whole existence has been torn apart. The roles you have always played no longer apply, and you are thrust into the unknown. It is natural to have identity crises at this period. Who are you now that you no longer have the identifying label of "spouse" or "partner"? Which ideals, goals, and hopes best represent who you really are?

Disclosing One's True Identity

Divorce may be a difficult time, but it can also be a time of profound personal growth. It is an opportunity to shed the persona you have been putting on for years, decades, and reveal the genuine self you have always been. Consider it a meeting with your authentic self, the one that may have been hiding away all this while.

It is like finding an old friend again, one whose ambitions, hobbies, and passions have been buried under the weight of marriage and parenthood. If you have put aside your true feelings, principles, and aspirations throughout your marriage, now is the moment to contact them. By delving into these facets, you set in motion the fundamental process of recreating your identity from the ground up.

Awakening Dormant Interests

As you explore your identity, you can rediscover old hobbies that have been buried under the pressures of married life. It is like discovering a treasure box in your own attic. Any number of activities, from making art and music to writing and reading to solving puzzles and playing sports, might fall under this category.

Maybe you used to be really enthusiastic about something, like a pastime or a field of study. After gaining your independence via a divorce, you will be able to revisit these interests with fresh eyes. Your dedication to these activities goes much beyond mere pastime. They have the power to renew your enthusiasm for life and give you a feeling of direction.

Taking Pride in One's Own Independence

After a divorce, reclaiming your individuality is a statement of independence. It is about making decisions that feel true to who you are as a person, rather than conforming to other people's standards or the roles you performed throughout your marriage. Discovering your own unique worth and having the freedom to make your own choices may be really powerful.

Keep in mind that you have many people rooting for you as you embark on your quest for self-discovery. The experiences of those who came before you should serve as sources of encouragement and motivation. They show that there is great opportunity for development and self-definition after divorce, even in the midst of turbulence and change.

Let us welcome this opportunity to rediscover who you are and what you are capable of and rejoice in the fact that you are an original among millions. It is an exciting time of growth and new beginnings, when you may decide how you want your life to unfold.

Personal growth stories after divorce

A divorce is a major life change that may rock your entire world. Uncertainty, emotional upheaval, and a deep feeling of loss characterize this trip. However, inside the fire of divorce, one might find an extraordinary chance for self-improvement and reinvention. In this article, we will look at the lives of people who have been through a divorce and come out on the other side stronger and more self-reliant.

Jennifer: Gaining Freedom Once Again

Jennifer's tale is an inspiring account of perseverance and personal growth. She was at a crossroads after her 15-year marriage ended in divorce. For the first time, she had trouble remembering what it was like to be a wife and mother. Jennifer set out on a quest to reacquaint herself with her autonomy and sense of self.

She began by going after a lifelong ambition to see the world. She found that traveling alone to far-flung places was the best way to reawaken her spirit of exploration and independence. She was always learning about herself and the world as she traveled. She gained the confidence to trust her judgment and experience the freedom that comes with deciding and acting on her own.

Divorce may be a catalyst for reinventing one's sense of self and restoring independence, as Jennifer's tale demonstrates. It is a chance to indulge in some self-discovery, follow those ambitions we have put on the back burner for too long, and enjoy the independence that comes with that.

David: Turning Suffering into Meaning

The process of David's divorce was fraught with intense suffering and personal turmoil. He had to cope with the emotional fallout of his divorce and the arduous task of co-parenting his two young children. This was a time of deep introspection.

David transformed his suffering into a driving sense of purpose with the help of treatment and encouragement from his loved ones. He began giving his time to a local charity that helps children whose parents are going through a divorce. He discovered a profound feeling of satisfaction in assisting others through the complicated process of divorce.

The events in David's life show that even the worst circumstances may lead to positive changes in one's character.

Through channeling his suffering into aid for others, he found strength and meaning in life.

Accepting Oneself (Natalie)

Intense self-criticism and self-blame characterized Natalie's experience of divorce. She just could not escape the notion that she was a bad wife and mother. It was not until she learned about self-compassion that she started to see things differently.

Natalie developed the ability to show herself the same compassion she would give to a close friend by engaging in self-compassion activities. She had come to terms with the fact that her divorce was but another part of her life's narrative. She was able to recover and adopt a more upbeat perspective after learning to show kindness to herself in this way.

Self-compassion may have a profound effect, as Natalie's experience shows. She discovered healing and a greater sense of self-acceptance and progress by showing herself compassion and understanding during the challenging process of divorce.

Passions Rekindled, by Jason

Jason's divorce gave him the freedom to pursue interests he had put on hold while he was married. Although he had always enjoyed music, he had to give it up to focus on his family. After he and his wife split up, he picked up his guitar and started writing songs again.

This reconnection to his artistic past filled him with immense satisfaction and meaning in life. Jason even started a band with like-minded individuals. He not only regained his passion for music, but also developed strong bonds with his collaborators.

Divorce, as Jason's experience shows, may help us rediscover our motivation for doing things we had forgotten we loved. It is a call to unleash our inner artists and express ourselves in whichever way speaks to you most.

Noel: Dedicated to Never Stop Learning

Noel had always wanted to continue her studies, but she got married and had to put that goal on hold. But following her divorce, she made the decision to put her own needs first. She decided to pursue a master's degree in an area that really interested her.

Noel's motivation and self-assurance grew as she immersed herself in her studies, and she learned new things as a result.

Investing in one's own development and sense of agency via continuing education became a priority.

Divorce, as Noel's experience shows, may be a catalyst for investing in one's own development as a person and as a thinker. It serves as a timely reminder that we should never stop learning and growing.

These examples of maturation show how divorce may lead to positive change. They serve as a poignant reminder that even in the face of tragedy and change, there is room for growth, fortitude, and personal agency.

Keep in mind that everyone's divorce experience is different, and there are many ways to find development after going through a breakup. Know that you may come out on the other side of divorce as a better, more powerful version of yourself if you put the effort into it. This might be via travel, community service, self-compassion, artistic expression, education, or anything else that inspires you.

The power of mindfulness

It might be difficult to maintain your equilibrium among the chaos of a divorce. The ups and downs of emotion, the unpredictability of the future, and the burden of the past may all work together to shake your serenity. Mindfulness, however, is a powerful method for obtaining peace of mind, recovering from trauma, and developing one's full potential.

Methods for Relaxation and Stress Reduction

Mindfulness is essentially an attitude toward life in which one lives in the present moment with undivided attention and acceptance of whatever arises. Mindfulness is the practice of paying attention to — but not getting caught up in — your internal experiences. This simple technique has the potential to profoundly alter your divorce experience and beyond.

Here are some ways to cultivate mindfulness and find calm within:

Concentrated breathing:

Mindful breathing is one of the easiest and most accessible ways to develop mindfulness. Relax with your eyes closed, your body at ease, and your concentration on your breathing for a time. Take a moment to focus on the feeling of breathing in and out. When your thoughts stray (and they will), bring them back to your breathing slowly and softly. Doing this often might help you relax and focus on the here and now.

Benefit of Meditating

Mindfulness is a skill that may be honed via regular meditation sessions. You may meditate by focusing on your breathing, a word or phrase (a mantra or scripture), or a guided meditation or prayer; all you need is a peaceful place and some time to yourself. Practicing meditation or praying regularly might help you become more in tune with yourself and find calm inside.

In-Body X-Ray

In a body scan, you focus your awareness on every area of your body, from your toes to your brain. Keep an eye out for areas of tension or pain while you do this. You may improve your awareness of and connection with your body with this technique.

Walking with awareness

Spend some time strolling in the great outdoors, a nearby park, or even your own neighborhood. Focus on your surroundings while you walk, including the sensation of the earth under your feet. Mindful walking is a great approach to ground oneself in the here and now while also releasing tension.

Compassion for oneself

Mindfulness is more than just paying attention to the here and now; it also requires being kind to oneself. Think of yourself as a friend and be as patient and gentle with yourself as you would be with them. When difficult feelings develop, it is important to accept them without condemning yourself and to speak kind words to yourself.

Letting go and accepting what is

Meditation on the present moment, including one's feelings and thoughts, is called "mindfulness." It is not about trying to stuff or ignoring negative emotions, but rather, gently recognizing and accepting them. Doing so may help you let go of painful feelings and make room for restoration.

Techniques for achieving inner peace

Mindfulness provides a wealth of strategies to explore in your search for inner peace among the difficulties of a divorce. We have discussed several helpful ways for finding calm in the middle of life's storms, but here are some more to consider.

A Meditative Practice with Sound

In the practice of sound meditation, one pays close attention to one's internal and exterior auditory experiences. Relax in relative silence and tune in. Hear the wind in the trees, the birdsong, the hum of the appliances, and anything else that may seem inconsequential. Tune in to the beat of your heart or the rhythm of your breathing for a moment of peace and serenity. Developing a keener sense of hearing is one way this exercise might bring you closer to the here and now.

Relaxing Your Muscles One at a Time

Tense and then relax groups of muscles one by one to practice progressive muscle relaxation. One should begin from the feet and work their way up to the head. Feel the stress go away as you systematically relax every muscle in your body. Physical relaxation and mental peace are the results of this exercise.

Creative practice with awareness

One way to practice mindfulness is to engage in an artistic pursuit. Give yourself completely to whatever creative endeavor you are pursuing. Focus on the visual elements of your statement, such as hues, textures, and motion. The creative process has been shown to have calming and peaceful effects.

Variations on Mindful Breathing

Add some variety to your mindful breathing exercises. Try concentrating on the movement of your stomach up and down while you breathe deeply. Try out the method of breathing in through one nostril and out through the other, sometimes known as "alternate nostril breathing." The awareness of your breath may be increased, and relaxation can be facilitated by trying them out.

Mindfulness of Compassion

Loving-kindness sending forth positive vibes of love and kindness to oneself and others is at the heart of Metta meditation. Take a seat and mutter to yourself, "May I be happy. I pray for good health. I pray for a life of ease. Then, share your good vibes with everyone you know, from family and friends to casual acquaintances and even adversaries. By cultivating empathy, one may find contentment within oneself.

Being Here Now: A Place of Growth and Healing

Being mindful is not only about relaxing in the face of adversity; it is also about embracing every aspect of your life, good and bad. It may be used for self-improvement and recovery.

Mindfulness may help you better understand your feelings and mental processes. It is possible to strengthen your character in the midst of hardship, make choices that are in line with your principles, and find a contentment inside yourself that is independent of your marital status.

Comprehending Emotions and Thoughts

Understanding your own feelings and thinking processes is a cornerstone of mindfulness. Divorce may cause a roller coaster of emotions and thoughts, including doubt and confusion. Mindfulness gives you a soft yet perceptive understanding of these processes.

You may get a deeper understanding of your emotions by just watching them. Your emotional responses and the stories you've been telling yourself might be traced back to their origins. Understanding is just the beginning, however; this insight provides a bedrock for development and restoration.

Character Development via Adversity

Divorce is, without a question, a harrowing ordeal. It puts your fortitude, tolerance, and development potential to the test. By strengthening your moral fiber, mindfulness may help you rise to the challenge at hand.

Mindfulness is a terrific tool for becoming introspective and emotionally intelligent. As you develop a deeper understanding of your core beliefs, you will be better able to make choices that reflect who you really are. Your character and integrity will be strengthened by this inward alignment, allowing you to manage the challenges of divorce with poise and confidence.

Discovering Happiness From Within

The capacity to be happy with oneself regardless of one's marital situation is a deep benefit of practicing mindfulness. It teaches you that contentment is an internal condition that can be developed regardless of whether or not you have a romantic relationship.

The Road Ahead

Chapter 6 marks a new beginning, a clean slate in the post-divorce path. It is a new page where you may discover the fascinating possibilities and undiscovered areas of the road ahead. In this piece, we will talk about two crucial parts of moving on after a divorce: dating and making plans for the future.

After the emotional upheaval of a divorce has subsided, you may find yourself thinking about getting back out there and dating. There are many possible reactions to this subject, from enthusiasm to fear. In this article, we will use a combination of first-person experiences and professional guidance to help you successfully navigate the dating scene.

Now is a great moment to imagine the kind of future you want to have as you start this new phase of your life. In order to develop and achieve one's full potential, it is crucial to set objectives and dream big. Our goal is to help you identify your goals, no matter how large or little they may be, and then provide you with the tools you need to make them a reality.

As you go on to Chapter 6 of your life after divorce, keep in mind that this new chapter is a continuation of your tale, the one only you can create. If the future holds the possibility of fresh love or the pursuit of your deepest aspirations, you will be better prepared to welcome it with the insights and counsel provided in this chapter. A positive future awaits you as you move on from your divorce, which is a tribute to your strength, perseverance, and development potential.

Dating and Rediscovering Love

Finding love again after a breakup is an exciting and terrifying adventure. It is a new beginning, an invitation to re-enter the dating scene and see how things have evolved since you last tried them. Here, we will guide you down this route with a mix of personal experiences and professional counsel, so you may set off on this thrilling voyage with confidence and enthusiasm.

Dating again after a divorce is like starting a whole new novel, with endless possibilities for fulfillment. It is a chance to start again, building on the strengths you discovered in your prior partnership while also making use of the insights gained from your past experiences.

Stepping back into the world of relationships

Divorce might seem like a daring new experience when one enters the world of relationships for the first time. It is an important milestone on the road to self-discovery and development, leading to the possibility of deeper relationships down the road. In this article, we will delve into the many sides of this thrilling adventure, sharing advice and insights to help you go forward with optimism and confidence in your post-divorce relationships.

Embracing a Fresh Start

It is normal to feel both excited and nervous about the idea of dating again after going through a divorce. It is like being on the cusp of a whole new universe, where every contact has the potential to offer you happiness, belonging, and satisfaction. It is a fresh start, a chance to start again without holding onto any negative feelings or regrets.

Applying What We've Learned

You have probably learned a lot about yourself, your wants, and your ideal spouse from your past marriage. These realizations provide a firm basis for your future relationships, whether it is via better communication, the significance of creating healthy boundaries, or a deeper knowledge of your values and objectives. It is an opportunity to put one's learned expertise to use in building stronger, more meaningful relationships.

How to Date in the Digital Age

With the advent of the Internet came a number of new dating options for singles to explore. You may find dates in a variety of places, from online dating sites to parties to specialized meet ups. We will discuss the benefits and drawbacks of each strategy, allowing you to make an informed decision based on your unique needs and preferences.

Making Insightful Links

The capacity to connect on a deep level is the bedrock of every healthy friendship or romantic relationship. We will go into the fundamental concepts that support all kinds of relationships, whether you are looking for a platonic friend, a close buddy, or an enthusiastic partner. The foundations of trust and thriving relationships are open lines of communication, mutual regard, and emotional closeness.

Striking a Balance between Autonomy and Collaboration

Finding a happy medium between your need for solitude and the company of others is essential when you re-enter the dating scene. Rather than defining you, a healthy partnership should enrich your life. We will talk about how to keep your independence and yet make the deep relationships you want. Maintaining this equilibrium will allow you to forge connections with others that will improve your life.

Honoring the Path You've Taken

Your ability to heal, strengthen, and progress in the wake of your divorce is inspiring. It is a trip where you get to write the story, meet interesting people, and discover your own sense of purpose. Step back into dating with an adventurous spirit and the certainty that your own special tale has only just begun. Everything you do, everyone you meet, and everything you experience becomes a thread in the rich tapestry of your life story. Welcome this next phase with excitement and optimism, knowing that it may lead to exciting new experiences and rewarding connections.

Personal anecdotes and expert advice

Personal experiences and professional guidance might help you find your way back to love and connection after a divorce. They provide unique viewpoints, common experiences, and useful advice to help you confidently and wisely face this new and exciting chapter in your life.

The Influence of One's Own Experiences

Anecdotes from real people's experiences are like glimpses into their worlds. They provide insights into the lives of those who have explored the realm of relationships after divorce, including their achievements, struggles, and lessons learned. These accounts illuminate the path ahead and remind us that we are not alone.

You could find yourself relating to the stories of others who have gone through similar situations. Their experiences provide light on future prospects and provide guidance for negotiating the intricacies of romantic relationships. Most significantly, they assure you that this new phase of your life may really bring you joy and satisfaction.

Professional Advice for Making the Right Decisions

Expert guidance is just as important as personal anecdotes when it comes to helping you make decisions about your romantic life. Professionals in the fields of psychology and counseling may provide light on the complexities of contemporary dating, making meaningful connections, and maintaining satisfying relationships.

Relationship experts provide guidance on a broad variety of issues, including how to communicate clearly, how to establish healthy boundaries, and how to prioritize self-care. It gives you the background and skills you need to approach interpersonal interactions with awareness and compassion, paving the way for a life of enrichment and development.

You will get a complete picture of life after divorce through the mix of first-hand accounts and professional guidance. It is a potent combination of personal insight and expert knowledge that allows you to make decisions that are in line with your ethics, goals, and dreams.

Personal stories

- **Emily's Struggle to Find Herself:**

Emily's life has reached a crossroads after her divorce. She felt a need for adventure and self-discovery after devoting so many years to her husband and raising her children. She made the decision to rediscover the joy she had felt for nature when she was younger.

Emily decided to join a local hiking club in an effort to contact nature and, by extension, with herself. She met Daniel on a strenuous journey through beautiful terrain. He was a kind fellow hiker, and his excitement for the mountains was contagious. Conversations flowed easily as they made their way together across challenging terrain and gorgeous scenery.

Each new experience brought them closer together. Daniel listened sympathetically as Emily described her process of coming into her own after her divorce. Nature's ability to mend broken hearts was not foreign to him. The outdoors became a potent metaphor for their blossoming romance, which was like an adventure full of highs and lows and the prospect of fresh beginnings.

As time went on, their friendship blossomed into a love as unforced as the environments they discovered together. Emily finally felt at rest and whole for the first time in years thanks to Daniel. Theirs was a love forged in the peaceful splendor of the mountains, a testimony to the restorative power of the natural world and the resilience of the human heart.

- The Story of Rachel and Mike

The narrative of Rachel and Mike was one of reunion after a long separation. They were high school sweethearts who had been torn apart by unexpected turns of fate. They were both single parents who had been through the anguish of divorce.

They were reunited via social media, of all places. Rachel got a friend request from Mike one day, and it brought up a lot of old memories. They went from chatting online to meeting in person swiftly and seemed to immediately feel like old friends.

It was clear that their bond was stronger than ever as they recounted their experiences together after the breakup. Something deep had been reignited, and it was evident in the laughing, the ease of discussion, and the old comfort of each other's company. Their friendship developed into a strong and fulfilling relationship over time.

Rachel and Mike's tale shows that first loves can last and that second chances do exist. Along the way, they had a tremendous feeling of familiarity, like the spark between them was reignited from when they were young. It was as if fate had brought them back together to show them that real love can last forever.

- Max's Efforts to Better Himself

After his divorce, Max felt lost and confused about who he was. He made the decision to focus his efforts on developing his own character. He found that therapy was crucial in his recovery, equipping him to deal with the emotional fallout of his separation and divorce.

Max made the concurrent decision to broaden his horizons and rediscover long-lost interests. He sought solace and self-awareness so he enrolled in a program on mindfulness meditation. There he met Olivia, who was also taking part in a program designed to promote health and personal growth.

During their first chats together, they spoke up about the challenges they had faced after their separation. Max respected Olivia's determination to better herself. He felt a connection to her serene demeanor and generosity of heart.

They became closer as a result of their mutual dedication to introspection and development. Together, they overcame the obstacles on their paths and inspired one another throughout. Their romance was an example of the transformational power of introspection and the possibility of love blossoming when we least expect it.

These stories of second chances at love after divorce highlight the power of self-improvement and the surprising ways in which love may enter our lives. They serve as a constant reminder that we may discover love in the most unexpected places and at the most unexpected moments, and that when it does, it can offer us a fresh sense of purpose and pleasure in life.

Setting Goals and Dreaming Big

Divorce is a major life change that causes many people to go within and reevaluate their priorities and objectives. In this section, we will talk about how crucial it is to envisage a bright future for yourself following divorce, complete with new objectives and aspirations. It is a chance to map out a future that is in harmony with who you really are and will offer you joy and satisfaction.

Creating a New Roadmap

When a marriage ends in divorce, it is the beginning of a new chapter. It is an opportunity to start again, unfettered by the baggage of a previous commitment. It is important to think about what matters most to you as you go forward on this trip.

Choosing What's Most Important

Establish what matters most to you first. Where do your priorities lie? It might be anything from developing oneself to moving up the corporate ladder to investing in meaningful relationships to following one's true calling. The first step in achieving any significant objective is to determine what those priorities are.

Goal-setting using the SMART framework

Goals should be SMART (Specific, Measurable, Achievable, Relevant, and Time-bound) once you have established your priorities. Your ambitions will gain focus and form as a result of using the SMART framework. If you want to improve yourself, a SMART goal may be to take a class or attend a workshop during the next six months to hone your expertise in a certain field.

Optimistic Hopes

When you give yourself permission to dream large, you enable yourself to imagine a future that extends beyond your current circumstances. It is about having the courage to see a future that fills you with boundless happiness and contentment. Your aspirations may concern many different areas of your life, including work, relationships, self-improvement, and even travel.

Getting Past Self-Limiting Beliefs

It is freeing to dream large, but often such dreams come with self-defeating assumptions. Past experiences and self-doubt are common sources of these assumptions. Recognizing and questioning such false ideas is crucial, as is replacing them with more constructive and optimistic ones.

Envisioning the future after divorce

You have reached a turning point in your life after your divorce, a place where the past is in the past and the future is a blank canvas ready to be filled with your goals and ideas. Introspection, goal setting, and a deep dive into what means most to you—all are key components of the art of future-planning, which we will discuss in detail below.

Page Turning

An important part of your life may close when you get a divorce. Even though you may be feeling the effects of loss and transition, now is the perfect moment to start a whole new story — one that you get to create. As you prepare to step into the next chapter of your life, keep in mind that you write the ending.

How to Find Your True North

The first step in creating a future you are excited about is finding your North Star. To get started, think about what is most important to you in life, what excites you, and what you value. Think back on the times and places when you felt the most alive and satisfied. These musings will guide you toward discovering what you value most in life.

Putting Together Your Plan

Knowing what you value most, you may set out to create your future vision. Think about the sort of relationships, job, and way of life that will fulfill your hopes and dreams. Permit yourself to dream wildly, to see a future that is better than you could have imagined.

Creating Measurable Objectives

When a vision is converted into manageable chunks, it may be put into motion. Goals should be SMART (Specific, Measurable, Achievable, Relevant, and Time-bound) in order to be effective. Having a plan with specific and attainable objectives helps you get closer to your end goal.

Defeating Obstacles

There might be obstacles to future planning, such as self-limiting beliefs or a fear of the unknown. It is critical to recognize these challenges and work to overcome them. Use affirmations and the help of friends or a coach to overcome self-doubt, and keep in mind that the most significant personal development takes place just outside people's comfort zones.

Taking Things Slowly

Each step you take brings you closer to your future goals. Just do a little at a time and you will get there. Your progress toward the future you have imagined is incremental but steady.

Keeping Your Options Open

It is impossible to forecast the future, and anything may happen in life. It is important to have an open mind while you work to make your idea a reality. Maintain a flexible outlook and welcome new possibilities that fit your core beliefs.

The Slate Is Empty

Inspiration and understanding may be found in the experiences of those who have begun the process of reimagining their lives following divorce. These anecdotes show that everyone has their own, unique way to a successful future, and that the options are almost endless.

Practical steps to achieve new dreams

It is exciting to think about what you want your life to be like in the future and make plans for it, but it will take demanding work and a well-thought-out strategy to make that future a reality. Here, we will discuss some of the concrete actions you may take after your divorce to move toward your ideal future.

Clearly define your objectives

Setting well-defined objectives is the first step in realizing your ambitions. Your objectives should be specific, attainable, and consistent with your long-term vision. If you want to change careers, one possible objective is to get a new certification as quickly as possible.

Make a Plan of Action

Once you know what you want, you can make a plan that will get you there. Make your long-term objectives into shorter, more doable objectives. Having a plan laid out in front of you is like having a beacon guiding you.

Learn as much as you can

Learning new things is a prerequisite for achieving many people's aspirations. The pursuit of a new profession or the launch of a new firm frequently necessitates a commitment to lifelong learning. If you want to improve your skills, look into taking classes, attending seminars, or finding a mentor.

Connect and network

Having a network and a group of supporters behind you may be a huge help on your path to success. Get involved in professional associations, go to networking events, and meet others with similar goals. These bonds have the potential to be sources of direction, openings, and consolation.

Take control of your schedule

Finding a happy medium between family, career, and personal goals may be difficult. Time management skills are crucial. Plan up your week so that you may make progress on your objectives while also giving yourself time to relax and enjoy life.

Persevere in the Face of Adversity

Be prepared for challenges. It is an inevitable part of getting anywhere. Put your energy into finding solutions to problems and being resilient. Get the help you need from your friends and famil and remind yourself why you want to achieve your goals.

Mark Important Dates

Rejoice in your successes, no matter how little they may appear at the time. Acknowledging your successes along the way is a terrific way to keep your spirits up and keep moving forward.

Maintain Flexibility

Modularity is a desirable trait. If things change or new chances present themselves, do not be rigid about sticking to your original plan. Being flexible helps you handle life's curveballs with ease.

Retain Your Dedication and Perseverance

After a divorce, it may require more time and work to realize your goals. Do not give up on your goals no matter how tough things become. The difference between successful and unsuccessfu is largely a matter of stubbornness.

Advice from Experts

Sometimes you need the help of an expert to make your aspirations come true. Do not be shy about consulting specialists for help, whether it is in the form of financial assistance, career counseling, or legal representation.

You may continue working steadily toward your goals after a divorce by following these steps and being committed to your vision. Keep in mind that you are on a trip unlike any other, and that it may take unexpected turns. Accept where you are at this moment, be strong, and keep your sights set on your aspirations.

Chapter 7

Embracing the New You

The new you has emerged after the divorce, and this chapter is a celebration of that. In this article, we will discuss the amazing process of gaining autonomy and using one's imagination as a means of self-healing.

If you are ready to start over and embrace your freedom, a divorce might be more than simply the end of your marriage. It is a time to be proud of your independence and the decisions you have made that are in line with who you want to be.

The therapeutic and cathartic effects of creative expression cannot be overstated. This section will show you how participating in creative activities may be therapeutic and transforming, whether you are an artist, writer, musician, or have never explored your creative side before.

Keep in mind that the process of being comfortable with the new you is one of self-discovery and self-love. It is a chance to strike out on your own, unleash your inner artist, and revel in your specialness.

Let us approach this section with an adventurous spirit and an open mind. The freedom to express oneself and the healing power of art are two themes we will investigate together. This section will help you make the most of the many doors that will open to you on your journey forward after your divorce.

Embracing Independence

A new day brings with it the possibility of gaining independence and freedom. Divorce is the beginning of an exciting new chapter in your life, one in which you may finally embrace your individuality and live life on your own terms.

Celebrating newfound autonomy and freedom

At its heart, independence is a time to honor one's individuality. It is an opportunity to celebrate the growth you have experienced as an individual apart from the roles you have played in the past, such as husband or partner. It is an adventure in which you rediscover your likes, dislikes, and deepest wants. The richness of life lies in its many choices, and this chapter is a tribute to the freedom that comes with making your own decisions. In this article, we will discuss the many ways in which single adults might thrive after divorce.

The glory of independence

Self-determination's crowning achievement is its autonomy. To do this, you must accept responsibility for your own life and make choices based on your values and priorities. Autonomy gives you the freedom to put your own needs and desires first in all aspects of life, including professional and personal decisions.

Creating Your Own Special Road

One size does not fit all when it comes to freedom. Creating a life that serves your goals and ideals is the goal. It is an opportunity to go at your own speed and choose your own destination. Some people get their kicks out of exploring new interests, while others value the leeway to make decisions that are true to who they really are.

Stories of individuals thriving in independence

Divorce may be a significant turning point in one's life, an opportunity to rip apart the old and make way for the new. Finding your way as a single person after a divorce is not just about making it through; it is about thriving, flourishing, and accepting life in all its glorious completeness. Here, we will hear the motivational accounts of those who have not only accepted but flourished in their newfound freedom.

Please note that in order to protect the identities of those discussed in these accounts, certain facts and names have been changed.

Lena: Reconnaissance and Rediscovery

Lena's life changed drastically after her divorce. It was an opportunity to focus on herself again, after years of prioritizing her husband and their family. She began by picking up a paintbrush and canvas again and spent hours creating. What was first intended as a means of self-care quickly took on greater significance.

Lena finally decided to follow her lifelong ambition and become an artist. She staged her first solo show thanks to her doggedness and the encouragement of new acquaintances she made in art class. Sales aside, it was a momentous success since it gave her a feeling of direction and accomplishment in life. Lena's life is an inspiration for everybody who wants to rediscover their hobbies and create a meaningful future for themselves.

Alex: Creating an Exciting Future for Myself

Alex's divorce was the first step towards a new and exciting chapter of his life. Although he had always had a fervent desire to see the world, he seldom left the country after getting married. He was divorced and then chose to travel the globe to get over it.

A quest Alex set out on led him to far-flung places on Earth. He trekked through verdant jungles, admired historic temples, and made friends from many walks of life. He came to appreciate the world's beauty and his own resiliency during his travels.

What started out as an adventure on one's own quickly became a way of life. Alex currently maintains a blog in which he advises and inspires other travelers. His experiences show that striking out on one's own may lead to rewarding discoveries and adventures.

Sophie Is Doing Great as A Sole Proprietor

Significant financial difficulties arose for Sophie as a result of her divorce. She had to make ends meet for her family of four on a little salary. Sophie did not let this setback make her give up on her goals of starting her own business.

Sophie, who had a natural talent for baking, opened a modest shop out of her kitchen. The reputation for baking delicious goodies quickly spread across the neighborhood. What was started as a means to make ends meet flourished into a successful enterprise? Sophie's narrative exemplifies the strength and originality that may emerge when one values freedom for its own sake.

Divorce is difficult, but these accounts show that it can also be a source of personal development and satisfaction. We hope that the stories of Lena, Alex, and Sophie will encourage you to follow your own unique route to self-sufficiency, the pursuit of your interests, and the creation of a life that speaks to your deepest values and deepest sense of who you are as a person. Your life is another example of perseverance and boundless possibility.

Healing Through Creativity
Creativity is like a thread that runs through the whole of our lives. It is the medium for expressing our innermost feelings, the soundtrack to our ups and downs, and the vehicle for our most profound ideas. Divorce may be traumatic, but this creative outlet can help you recover and express yourself in healthy ways.

An Effective Medicine: Art
Art, in all its manifestations, has a remarkable curative power. It helps you work through difficult sentiments, let go of pent-up

emotions, and find comfort in expressing yourself creatively. Participating in artistic pursuits can be a life-altering experience for everyone, whether they are seasoned artists or have never picked up a paintbrush before.

The Impact of Artistic Activity
Art is a language unto itself. You may convey the inexpressible, give meaning to the meaningless, and delve into the depths of your own mind with it. You may express yourself freely and contact your innermost thoughts and feelings when you engage in artistic pursuits like music, writing, or visual art.

A Releasing Therapeutic
The act of making art may be therapeutic. You may feel free to express yourself, face your concerns, and revel in your successes. You could learn something new about yourself and find some latent abilities.

Keeping a Journal for Introspection
Writing in a diary is one of the easiest ways to express your creativity. Writing down your thoughts and feelings might help you understand where you have been emotionally and where you want to go in terms of your recovery. It is an intimate setting where you can relax and be genuine.

Visual Arts, including Painting

Those who are artistically inclined may find release from their feelings via painting or sketching. The colors you choose, the strokes you make, and the pictures you draw may help you express yourself and let go.

Healing with Sound and Music

The ability of music to both calm the mind and excite the spirit is undeniable. Music may be a therapeutic companion whether you are producing tunes, playing an instrument, or just listening to the music you love.

Movement and Dance

Physical activity and dance both allow you to express your emotions via movement. You may feel your body relax, your mind clear, and your spirit soar all at once.

Taking the Creative Process at Face Value

Keep in mind that there are no limits or standards here as you discover the healing potential of art. Your artistic adventure is one of a kind, and it is a chance to contact your true self, let go of the past, and start over.

Conclusion

As you reach the last page of "Embracing Your Divorce," stop and think about how far you have come on this incredible trip. It has been a voyage of self-improvement, perseverance, and rediscovery, a demonstration of the power inside you.

Divorce is a turning moment that may drastically change the course of your life. Along the way, you have learned to understand and work with your feelings, negotiated the nuances of interpersonal relationships, and realized the significance of self-acceptance and love. You have cherished your freedom, fostered your imagination, and honored your individuality.

At this crossroads, you are holding the map to your future. The future is a blank slate onto which to inscribe your hopes and desires; a clean slate upon which to splash your most vivid artistic visions. It is a fresh start, a chance to author your own story and do anything you want with your life.

Your perseverance throughout this ordeal is an inspiration. You have turned your struggles into opportunities for personal development and improvement, and now you are stronger than ever. Your experience exemplifies the resilience of the human spirit and the potential for growth in the face of uncertainty.

Keep in mind that your life is a rich tapestry of struggles and successes. This is a tale about coming into one's own, developing one's character, and forging on with an unyielding will. As you put this book down, remember that your own personal story is only the beginning and will develop more with each passing day.

Have faith in yourself and your decisions as you go ahead. Make use of all you have experienced up to this point, from the knowledge you have received to the people who have helped you along the way. Think of today as a chance to learn, make new friends, and achieve your goals.

Your story has the ability to motivate and encourage those going through the uphill battle that is divorce. Help others on their own journeys toward wholeness and rebirth by sharing your experience, wisdom, and perseverance.

For those going through a divorce, "Embracing Your Divorce" is more than just a book; it is a friend, a guide, and a reminder that you are not alone. As you close this book, take heart in the knowledge that your life is only the beginning, full of exciting possibilities and the bonds of friendship that will last a lifetime.

Go forward with confidence, honor the path that only you can take, and let your brilliance shine. The beauty of your ever-evolving tale and the force of your unyielding soul shine a light on your way.

Honor your inner fortitude, your ability to bounce back, and the path that led you to become the exceptional person you are today. Your experience exemplifies the resilience of the human spirit and the potential for renewal and renewal. Keep going because you have the strength to see you through.

Helpful Suggestions for Going through a Divorce

Although the time spent in grieving will be difficult, there are steps you may do to ease the burden. The following are some insightful comments and recommendations. Take some time out to read them again. Throughout the remainder of the journey, several of these will be highlighted.

- Recognize your defeat.
- Express your discomfort aloud.
- Stop daydreaming and open yourself up to what really is.
- Like a roller coaster, your emotions will go up and down.
- You will be okay.
- Take it easy.
- Limit the number of key choices you make.
- To seek solace is quite acceptable.
- If you feel overwhelmed, reach out for help from people you know.
- Observe nature and spend time with animals Focus on what's important to you.
- Plan or prepare ahead of time for fun activities on days that tend to be stressful (such as your birthday or wedding anniversary).
- Negative emotions are temporary.

Feel the pain; don't try to numb it.

It's helpful to pray.

Made in the USA
Columbia, SC
10 March 2024

32376053R00068